Sey_our _imon

SEE
MORE
READERS

KILLER

This book is dedicated to my wife, Joyce.

Special thanks to reading consultant Dr. Linda B. Gambrell, Director of the School of Education at Clemson University, past president of the National Reading Conference, and past board member of the International Reading Association.

Permission to use the following photographs is gratefully acknowledged:
front cover: © Jeanne White, Photo Researchers, Inc.; title page, pages 4–5: © Marilyn Kazmers/Dembinsky Photo Assoc. Inc.; pages 2–3, 10–11: © Tom McHugh, Photo Researchers, Inc.; pages 6–7: © Art Wolfe, Photo Researchers, Inc.; pages 8–9: © Patrick J. Endres/Visuals Unlimited; pages 12–13: © David B. Fleetham/Visuals Unlimited; pages 14–15: © Gregory Ochocki, Photo Researchers, Inc.; pages 16–17, 32: © Tom & Pat Leeson, Photo Researchers, Inc.; pages 18–19: © Tom Myers, Photo Researchers, Inc.; pages 20–21: © Bruce Frisch, Photo Researchers, Inc.; pages 22–23: © George D. Lepp, Photo Researchers, Inc.; pages 24–29: © Brandon Cole; pages 30–31: © Jerry McCormick-Ray, Photo Researchers, Inc.

First published in the United States by SeaStar Books, a division of North-South Books Inc., New York. Published simultaneously in Canada, Australia, and New Zealand by North-South Books, an imprint of Nord-Süd Verlag AG, Gossau Zürich, Switzerland.

Library of Congress Cataloging-in-Publication Data is available.
ISBN 1-58717-141-4 (reinforced trade edition)
1 3 5 7 9 RTE 10 8 6 4 2
ISBN 1-58717-142-2 (paperback edition)
1 3 5 7 9 PB 10 8 6 4 2
PRINTED IN SINGAPORE BY TIEN WAH PRESS
For more information about our books, and the authors and artists who create them,
visit our web site: www.northsouth.com

Killer whales are big, fast, and beautiful.

The large males are bigger than elephants and as fast as sharks.

Killer whales often leap clear out of the water. Killer whales are exciting to watch and learn about.

Killer whales are hunters.

But they do not attack people.

Killer whales eat mainly fish,

seal, squid, and penguin.

They also hunt dolphins

and other kinds of whales.

Many people call the killer
whale an orca.

Orca is the name scientists use.

Killer whales are found in
all the oceans of the world.

Most of them live in
the icy waters around
the North or South poles.

An orca looks like a large fish.

But it is not a fish.

It does not have gills

to help it breathe.

Instead, an orca breathes through a blowhole on the top of its head. And it has lungs like dogs, cats, and people. An orca can hold its breath for ten minutes or longer.

A female orca is nearly 20 feet long.

That's as long as an ambulance.

A male orca is a few feet longer.

It weighs up to ten tons.

That's as heavy as two elephants.

Orcas are good swimmers.
They can move through the
water at 30 miles per hour.
That's faster than you can run.

Orcas use their tails,
called flukes, for power.
They use flippers to steer
and to turn.

A male orca has a large, pointed fin on top of its body. These dorsal fins are up to six feet high. A female has a smaller, curved dorsal fin. The dorsal fin keeps a whale steady when it swims fast.

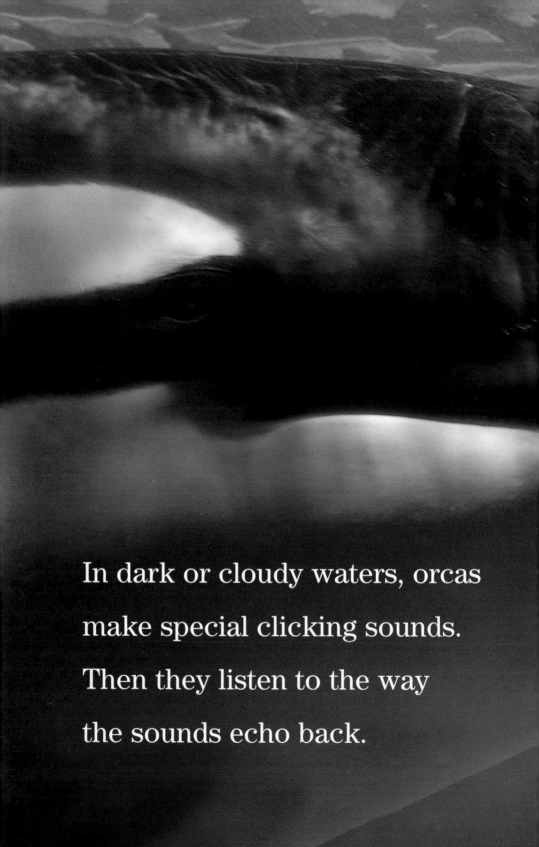

In dark or cloudy waters, orcas make special clicking sounds. Then they listen to the way the sounds echo back.

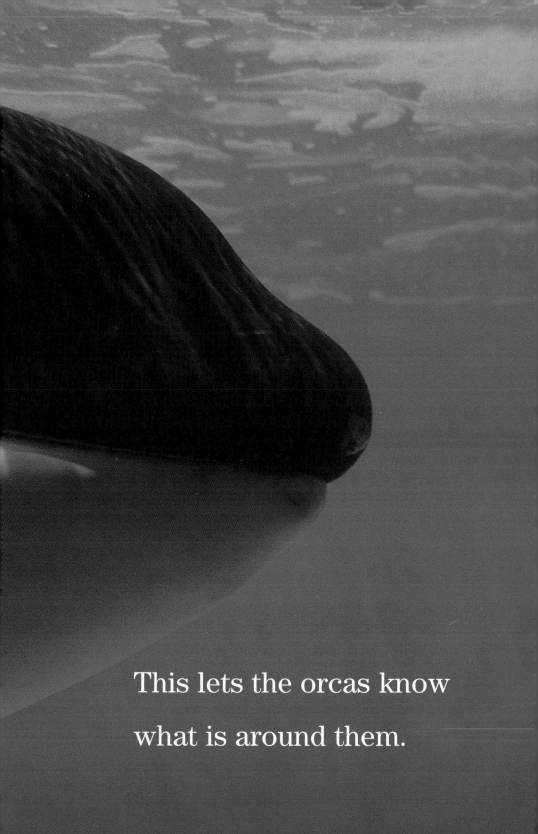

This lets the orcas know
what is around them.

Orcas have sharp, three-inch-long teeth for hunting.

Like wolves, orcas hunt in packs. They circle and herd their prey before attacking.

Orcas live in family groups
called pods.
The members of a pod hunt
and feed together.
They protect one another.

Some pods have fewer
than 10 whales.
Other pods have as many
as 50 whales.

Female orcas are called cows.
Male orcas are called bulls.
Baby orcas are born under water, near the surface.

A newborn orca calf
is eight feet long.
It weighs nearly 400 pounds.

A mother orca
nurses its calf
with milk.
Calves begin eating fish
and other foods at about
four months of age.
In one year the calf will grow
to be ten feet long and weigh
more than 1,000 pounds.

Orcas can leap high into the air.
Then they land back in the water
with a big SPLASH!
This is called breaching.

Most people do not see killer whales in the wild. They watch them in marine life parks, where orcas are often the star performers.

Scientists also study orcas in these parks.

They have found that orcas learn quickly.

Much about orcas
remains a mystery.
But as we learn more about orcas,
we gain a better understanding
of all wild animals.

KILLER WHALES • Spy Hop

Largest member of the dolphin family

Female weight: 3,000 to 8,000 pounds

Male weight: 8,000 to 12,000 pounds

Female length: 16 to 19 feet

Male length: 19 to 22 feet

Published by SeaStar Books, a division of North-South Books Inc.
Photograph © Marilyn Kazmers/Dembinsky Photo Assoc. Inc.

KILLER WHALES • Open Wide

Number of teeth: 40 to 50

Teeth length: 3 inches

Teeth width: 1 inch

Daily diet: 300 pounds of food

Swallows small seals
    and walruses whole

Published by SeaStar Books, a division of North-South Books Inc.
Photograph © Bruce Frisch, Photo Researchers, Inc.

KILLER WHALES • Leap

Top speed: 30 miles per hour

Average speed: 2 to 6 miles per hour

Can hold its breath for up to 10 minutes

Diving length: 1 to 4 minutes

Diving depth: 100 to 200 feet

Published by SeaStar Books, a division of North-South Books Inc.
Photograph © Marilyn Kazmers/Dembinsky Photo Assoc. Inc.

KILLER WHALES • Cow and Calf

Birth weight: 300 to 400 pounds

Average birth length: 8 feet

Growth rate first year: 4 inches per month

Weight gain first year: 1,000 pounds

First teeth: 4 months old

Published by SeaStar Books, a division of North-South Books Inc.
Photograph © Brandon Cole